Johnny Appleseed

By Christin Ditchfield

Consultant
Jeanne Clidas, Ph.D.
National Reading Consultant
and
Professor of Reading, SUNY Brockport

Children's Press ®
A Division of Scholastic Inc.
New York   Toronto   London   Auckland   Sydney
Mexico City   New Delhi   Hong Kong
Danbury, Connecticut

Designer: Herman Adler Design
Photo Researcher: Caroline Anderson
The photo on the cover shows Johnny Appleseed planting apple trees.

Library of Congress Cataloging-in-Publication Data

Ditchfield, Christin.
  Johnny Appleseed / by Christin Ditchfield.
     p. cm. — (Rookie biography)
Summary: Presents a brief biography of John Chapman, the man who planted
thousands of apple seeds in the early nineteenth century.
  ISBN 0-516-22853-6 (lib. bdg.)   0-516-27816-9 (pbk.)
  1. Appleseed, Johnny, 1774-1845—Juvenile literature. 2. Apple
growers—United States—Biography—Juvenile literature. 3. Frontier and
pioneer life—Middle West—Juvenile literature. [1. Appleseed, Johnny,
1774-1845. 2. Apple growers.] I. Title. II. Series.
  SB63.C46 D58 2003
  634'.11'092—dc21

                          2002015157

  3 4 5 6 7 8 9 10 R 12 11 10 09 08 07 06

Take a bite out of a big, juicy apple. Inside, you'll find a few tiny black seeds.

They may not look like much, but those little seeds can grow into a forest of trees. Just ask the man nicknamed "Johnny Appleseed."

His real name was John Chapman. John Chapman was born on September 26, 1774, on his family's farm in Leominster, Massachusetts. They lived in this cabin.

8

John Chapman liked to play by himself when he was a young boy. He went for long walks in the forest. He carefully studied the plants and animals that he found.

He left his home many years later. He traveled to the Ohio River Valley (VAL-ee).

He planted apple trees all
over the valley.

Chapman often went barefoot, even in the winter. He wore old clothes and carried a sack of apple seeds.

13

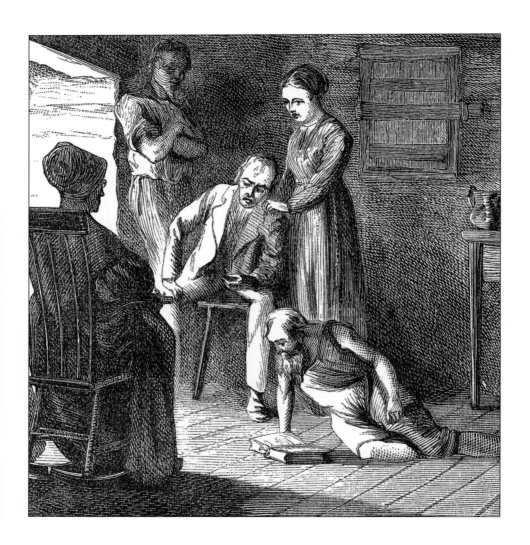

14

Families started moving into
the valley. Chapman visited these
settlers. He was kind and friendly.
He read to them from the Bible.
It was his favorite book.

Chapman taught the settlers everything he knew about the land. He helped them plant their own apple trees.

18

The settlers felt grateful to have these special trees. They were easy to plant and easy to pick. The settlers could eat the tasty fruit all year long.

The children could not wait for Chapman to visit! They called him "Johnny Appleseed."

Johnny Appleseed loved to laugh. He told the best stories. He always had time to play.

21

22

People said that Chapman was a friend to every living creature, "whether bear or wolf or rattlesnake or wasp."

Like the Native Americans, he knew how to make medicines from the plants that grew in the valley. He used these medicines to help people who were sick.

25

Chapman traveled from place to place for fifty years. He planted apple seeds in Connecticut, Massachusetts, New York, Pennsylvania, Ohio, and Indiana.

He died in Fort Wayne, Indiana,
when he was 70 years old.

John Chapman fed thousands of people with his wonderful apple trees.

A sign at his birthplace reads: "He planted seeds that others might enjoy fruit."

Words You Know

John Chapman

barefoot

cabin

forest

medicine

Ohio River Valley

seeds

settlers

31

Index

About the Author

Christin Ditchfield is an author, conference speaker, and host of the nationally syndicated radio program, *Take It to Heart!* A former elementary school teacher, Christin has written more than twenty books for children and on the topics of sports, science, and history. She lives in Sarasota, Florida.

Photo Credits

Photographs © 2003: Corbis Images: 14, 18, 31 bottom right (Bettmann), 10, 31 top right (Kevin Fleming), 13, 30 top right; Johnny Appleseed Visitor Center, Route 2, Leominster/Heidi Getek: 5; Leominster Historical Society: 7, 27, 30 bottom left, 30 top left; North Wind Picture Archives: cover, 8, 11, 30 bottom right; Photo Researchers, NY: 3 (Richard Hutchings), 4, 31 bottom left (James Welgos), 29 (Michael Newman).

Illustrations by Rodica Prato
Map by Bob Italiano